Open Windows

Open Windows

Craig Scott

craigsharley21@yahoo.com

ISBN 9798362615246

Edited and designed by Tell Tell Poetry

Printed in the United States of America

First Printing, 2022

Contents

Acknowledgments

I would like to thank Tell Tell Poetry for making my dream a reality. I also would like to thank my wife, Anita, who was with me through my endeavors from beginning to end. Lastly, I'd like to thank all my family for all of their support and encouragement.

Open Windows

The River Crossing

We all gather at the river's edge contemplating the right time to step in.
Fighting the currents and slippery rocks, sunbathing hippos and two-ton crocs—
if not now, when?
One by one we jump in knowing the river will take its toll. To some
it will be too late, and some will meet their fate from the jaws of the
croc death roll.
I can see the other side, almost there, can't look back! Hearing the
splashing of my fellow zebra gasping from the vicious, bloody attack.
Our hearts beat fast, not knowing how long this will last. I must
continue to move my legs, my body exhausted, my focus—I almost
lost it,
but now I can feel the bottom's edge.
I made it to the other side and must finish this great migration which I
began.
Six months later I will again face the gators and cross the river all over
again.

Never Stop Believing

Dad comes in my room to wake me up.
My day starts at 5, sun just starts to rise,
I have chores to do, no ifs, ands, or buts.
We have forty acres and a mule,
I feed the hogs, milk the cow, adjust the harness for the plow, all before going to school.
This was a way of life for former slaves, we hunt
what we eat, four to a bed when we slept,
but well-mannered and behaved.
It was common for whites to come around every now and then,
threaten to take our land, scare tactics from the Klan, but we stood our ground and would not give in!
At the end of the day, Grandma would gather to pray that God would keep us safe as we slept.
Papa would stay up sitting in his rocking chair, shotgun in hand with a blank stare.
Our safety was his to keep.
We have a roof over our heads, forty acres of land,
blisters and calluses were normal for our hands.
We work hard for what we have, and feel grateful for what we got,
growing up with an outhouse bathroom and the rooster as our clock.
Wearing coveralls, straw hat, no socks, no shoes, and when all six kids took baths, the same bathwater was used.
Played outside all day long,
until Mama said, *Get in this house! It's night and evil is out, and the day is far gone.*
Never forget where you came from, always remember where you're going.
Have a plan for not what you can't, but what you can, and your dream will never stop growing!

My Beautiful Bride

As I wake up each morning as the sun begins to rise,
I thank God in every way. He sanctions this day to take you as my bride.
You support me in every endeavor and putting my needs first and not last,
holding me and consoling me, always looking to the future and not dwelling on the past.
The day I proposed is where it all began—
I loved you from the start, to this day you still have my heart,
it feels like I'm reliving that day all over again!
As my wife, you complete me in every possible way,
the way you understand, and, always esteeming your man, I will truly enjoy this day!

I N
R I

The Victory on the Cross

ACT I: THE SCOURGE

Can you imagine seeing Christ tied to a post?
While his body prepares for the pain, and the soldiers prepare to be
  drained from beating him, which they will enjoy the most.
They beat him with cat-o'-nine-tails,
which is a lash intertwined with bones and glass
and bits of spiked nails.
When the lash hits his back it takes off part of the skin,
over and over, again and again—one soldier gets tired so another steps in.
Blood covers the ground, and the sun is on the rise.
They knew he was innocent but could not look into his eyes.
Yet continued this horrific beating . . . and Jesus kept on bleeding . . .
  until he couldn't be recognized.

ACT II: THE CRUCIFIXION

Crucifixion is the cruelest way to die.
Having spikes driven through your feet and hands,
no assistance from ropes or bands, it seems death is slow to pass you by.
They mock him who they came to view,
trying to give him vinegar to quench his thirst, which only made it worse,
but he said, *Father, forgive them, for they know not what they do.*
He came down from heaven and was convicted, judged, and tried.
His lungs began to collapse, from the dead weight perhaps, which was
  a painful death before he died.
False accusations, without hesitation, from onlookers is what was heard.
A thorn crown, blood streaming down, but he didn't say a word.
God in heaven and all the glory of host,
looking down on his son,
for the sacrifices he had done,
before Jesus finally gave up the ghost.

ACT III: THE RESURRECTION

No grave could hold him down, not even death could keep him bound.
Mary and Martha were in disarray, seeing the stone was rolled away
  and his body nowhere to be found.
What a glorious sight, him standing in all white, with all power in his hand,
to be received on high by and by, but not as a mortal man.
Jesus died so no soul would be lost,
and I can be free, him living inside of me,
because of the Victory on the Cross!

Fisherman of the Sea

I see an old man headed for the sea.
Dressed in rain gear, he made it quite clear
the ocean is the enemy, but he shows no fear.
He climbs aboard his floating chariot to battle the sea and what it will behold.
He moves forward on the attack, wind to his face, sun to his back,
while the angry sea starts to unfold.
The sea raised its sword which was a thirty-foot wave!
The fisherman maneuvers his boat,
trying to keep it afloat,
knowing all along he might not be saved.
No matter how much the sea tossed and toiled,
in the end the fisherman would win and return home with the spoils.
As he pulls into port from his victorious war,
fishermen to meet, family to greet,
he sees a little boy standing next to a store.
The child looks at the man, then reaches for his hand,
and asks, *who you be?*
The fisherman looks at the child and bends down with a smile,
and whispers, *I'm the Fisherman of the Sea.*

The Beast from the East

Grey clouds fill the sky, and a calm is in the air—
no rain in sight, no wind to fight
means it's the beginning of a nightmare.
It came from the east,
this terrible beast,
with one thing on its mind:
to unleash its mighty wrath
and destroy everything in its path
and do all this in fifteen minutes' time.
When it's done devouring your land
and putting fear in every man,
it comes back again,
wrapped up in a two-hundred miles per hour wind.
Its long black funnel can reach the sky,
and with its terrible voice
it will make the choice: who will live and who will die.

Rebel Inside of Me

What do you see when you look at me?
I'm the opposite of what society wants me to be.
You stop and stare at the clothes I wear,
tattoos on my chest.
What I feel is what I express;
if you don't like it, I really don't care.
I want to live outside the box and take it to the next level.
You see grass as green, I see grass as yellow.
I want to climb the highest building and walk on the ledge,
then test my faith and walk over the edge.
But the ground does not taste my feet?
Gravity says, *that's not fair—*
how can he be suspended in air?
Could it have been you that jumped instead of me?
I want to go to Harvard and sit in the back and not the front of the class,
and raise my hand to every question that is asked.
Even though I don't know the answer, I'll try to sound polite.
I'm in the instructor's head, he's trying to figure out what I said,
and even though I'm wrong, in his mind, I'm right!
I have to admit, at one point I wanted to quit,
and give in to what society wanted me to be.
Life tried to play me for a fool—
I said no and bent every rule.
That's just the REBEL INSIDE OF ME.

Rewind

Can you imagine growing up in the deep, deep South?
No lights, no running water, and you have a shack for a house?
No playgrounds around, no stores to be found,
and you're surrounded by a bunch of woods—
then you awaken in the middle of the night, by a cross burning bright, men outside with white hoods.
Now I thought it was a dream, a nightmare, so it seemed,
so I went into the corner to hide.
Then I heard a man's voice, I knew then we had no choice as he ordered us to come outside.
They took the only father figure I had,
put a rope on a tree, smiled at me, and hanged the only man I knew as dad.
I was devastated, seeing my dad half-naked and castrated, mom was next which they debated,
no one around for at least a mile, take a knife, rape the wife,
and all this seen through the eyes of a child!
Growing up as a young man it was hard for me to understand
the reason for segregation.
I thought we were all human beings, so it seemed, but they thought we were not equal to their generation.
When I went to a restaurant I couldn't use the front door,
and when I got on the bus
in the back it's just us
sometimes my seat became the floor!
We had no civil rights,
went to separate schools, transportation was cars, for us it was worn out shoes,
and bathrooms marked Colored and White.
Their jobs which I hated, because they were located
in a nice office building.
Ours was at some lumber mill or some cotton or bean field,
which did not exclude our children.
Forty years past, but not the pain and not the hate,
it's hard for me to explain even harder for you to relate,

but the scars are still left in the back of my mind!
And when I see a young black,
his views misused and his manhood attacked?
Forty years have just been REWIND!

Vietnam Through the Eyes of a Vet

Nineteen was the average age
to fight in a war of another man's rage.
As I stand in rice paddies up to my waist,
the fear of war I'm starting to taste.
At this point my mind starts to uncoil.
Trying to find a hidden land mine
makes me think I'll never again touch American soil.
The day is gone and the night starts to unfold,
tripwire, gunfire is what's expected on a night patrol.
The night is filled with terror,
and there's no room for error,
you have to keep up, and you can't lag.
If you do, there's a bullet just for you,
and you'll go home not alive but in a body bag.
I cannot lie, each night I cry, and I ask myself: why?
These people are humans just like me,
difference is . . . I'm American and they are VC!
But as I look at my target through my high-powered scope,
finger on the trigger, one shot—I figure
I have to do it clean so he won't die slowly.
This is something I can't explain—
I'm going from reality to being insane!
But since you were not there you really don't care,
you don't even have a clue.
Our lives were shredded, in our bodies bullets were embedded,
for America, the red, the white, and the blue.
So next time you see a vet, you show respect,
because they were sent there by good Old Uncle Sam,
To fight in a war where no one kept score,
this place called Vietnam!

Thank You for Your Service

A knock at the door, which I wanted to ignore, the sad greetings when the door opens.
Servicemen in uniform, wife begins to mourn, and not the news I was hoping.
But let's rewind back during the 911 attack, when my child first joined the military.
He wanted to do his part, which tore our hearts, but our pain and sorrow he would carry.
Dear Mom and Dad, I love you and this is my prayer:
as I go into a foreign land with my brothers hand in hand, this is the weight I have to bear.
My job is to fight for country to subdue my enemy,
remembering the Soldier's Creed, knowing there's a need to protect all who follow me.
IED explodes! Leaving my men exposed, and bullets whiz by that could devise my fate.
I see my soldiers pinned down, enemies all around, but I do not hesitate!
I use my body as a human shield, knowing there is a chance I might be killed.
Because of my actions, and solitude satisfaction, those soldiers are alive today.
Except one, who was your son, and I wouldn't have had it any other way.
So no sad words, when you think of me; it was an honor to serve this country, you see!
So when you visit my gravesite, try hard not to fight back the tears of feeling so sad and nervous.
As you think of me every day, up in heaven I can hear you say,
Thank you for your service!

Clean Slate

God looked down on this sinful earth and saw the sins of man:
in all its girth, there was no worth, so destruction was his plan.
Jesus said, *Father, I will go, and sacrifice for this sinful generation.*
The one they will seek to kill, the one whose stripes will heal, for this cruel and sinful nation.
The one who will go out and preach the word,
raising the dead, feeding five thousand souls with fish and bread. The name of Jesus would finally be heard.
The one who washed the feet of those he loved,
to show his disciples, you must be mindful, these acts come from God above. Going out and healing the sick and the blind that could not see—
casting demons out those who were possessed, and they openly confessed:
Jesus, I serve and follow thee.
And with his blood our debt is paid:
no respect for his person—in the garden, disciples' desertion, even kissed the man that had him betrayed.
The one who will be kicked, slapped, whipped, attacked, accused, abused . . . they denied him, three times, not having his back.
Yet he said, *I will leave this heaven divine, and die for the sins of mankind, and come down and set the record straight.*
I will be the sacrificial lamb, for those who don't understand you now have a clean slate!

AM I NOT A MAN AND A BROTHER?

I Am a Black Man

I am a black man living young, wild, and free!
Until my land was invaded,
by the Anglo-Saxon which I hated,
'cause he brought me into slavery.
He took me to America on this overcrowded ship.
Put me in chains, changed my name, and introduce me to a whip.
Being a black slave was always a losing battle.
Surrounded by hate, nowhere to escape, and they sold our families at auctions like cattle!
1865, a day we thought we would never see,
we were no longer black slaves, but we were set free!
Putting behind the days of picking cotton,
not to mention the lynchings and beatings we shouldn't have gotten,
while the master is drinking a glass of sweet tea.
With a lazy grin, and hate filled within, he said, *you will be back working for me.*
Take a good look at my plantation.
You won't get very far with no pride! No skill! And no education!
No education? W.E.B. DuBois wrote black history
and was the first to graduate from Harvard University;
Thurgood Marshall, first black justice of the Supreme Court, this is something America can't dispute,
Patricia Harris, first black woman in the presidential cabinet,
and Booker T. Washington headed the Tuskegee Institute.
No pride? When a man will fight for our Civil Rights
among violent, angry, racist whites!
While KKK searches to bomb black churches, he's telling people about his dream?
About blacks and whites, coming together to make America that much better,
and to die for that was Dr. Martin Luther King!
No skill? Blacks were overshadowed in the military, and history books tried to shut the door

on blacks, such as Buffalo Soldiers, Tuskegee Airmen, and the soldiers form the 54th.
But we reopen history, we're not isolated in our own little cocoon,
we've got blacks working from NASA to the White House, we're even sending blacks to the moon.
So don't let nobody tell you you're nothing, you need to take a stand.
Think back on black history, then smile and say—Yes, I am a Black Man!

About the Author

Craig Scott is currently active-duty military, and he has been serving over twenty-three years for this country. Growing up in a rural part of northern California, he started writing poetry at a young age. Craig grew up writing his own poems for special occasions (Mother's Day, Easter, Father's Day) instead of buying a card from a store. Often, he was summoned to read his poetry for special events, such as church functions and poetry slams. He inherited this special gift from his mother, who wrote poetry as well.

www.ingramcontent.com/pod-product-compliance
Lightning Source LLC
La Vergne TN
LVHW020533160826
845677LV00015B/4032

* 9 7 9 8 3 6 2 6 1 5 2 4 6 *